JOHN BROWN'S BODY

STEPHEN VINCENT BENÉT

John Brown's Body

WITH ILLUSTRATIONS BY FRITZ KREDEL
AND WARREN CHAPPELL

RINEHART AND COMPANY, INC.

NEW YORK • TORONTO

Published simultaneously in Canada by
Clarke, Irwin & Company, Ltd., Toronto

★

Text copyright, 1927, 1928, by Stephen Vincent Benét

★

Illustrations copyright, 1954, by Rinehart & Company, Inc.

★

Printed in the United States of America
By The Haddon Craftsmen, Scranton, Pa.
All Rights Reserved

★

Library of Congress Catalog Card Number: 54-9619

TO MY MOTHER
AND TO THE MEMORY
OF MY FATHER

NOTE

As this is a poem, not a history, it has seemed unnecessary to me to encumber it with notes, bibliography, and other historical apparatus. Nevertheless—besides such original sources as the Official Records, the series of articles in Battles and Leaders of the Civil War, and the letters, memoirs, and autobiographies of the various leaders involved—I should like to acknowledge my indebtedness to Channing's The War for Southern Independence and McMaster's The United States Under Lincoln's Administration, to Oswald Garrison Villard's John Brown: A Biography Fifty Years After, to the various Lives of Lincoln by Lord Charnwood, Carl Sandburg, and Ida Tarbell and the monumental work of Nicolay and Hay, to Nathaniel Wright Stephenson's Abraham Lincoln: An Autobiography, and, finally, my very particular debt to that remarkable first-hand account of life in the Army of the Potomac, Four Brothers in Blue, by Captain Robert Goldthwaite Carter, from which the stories of Fletcher the sharpshooter and the two brothers at Fredericksburg are taken.

In dealing with known events I have tried to cleave to historical fact where such fact was ascertainable. On the other hand, for certain thoughts and feelings attributed to historical characters, and for the interpretation of those characters in the poem, I alone must be held responsible.

The account of the defeated Union army pouring into Washington after the first Bull Run is founded on a passage in Whitman's Specimen Days and Collect.

The Black Horse Troop is an entirely imaginary organization and not to be confused with the so-called Black Horse Cavalry. In general, no fictional character in the poem is founded upon a real person, living or dead.

On page 56, in the inscription written by John Brown for his own monument, the dates of the deaths of his two sons are incorrectly given. They are so given in the original manuscript, now in the possession of the Genealogical Society of Pennsylvania, and I have not felt at liberty to alter the original wording.

STEPHEN VINCENT BENÉT

Neuilly-sur-Seine, April, 1928

A note on the illustrations: The decorations and opening illustrations for this edition have been made by Fritz Kredel. The portraits are translations into line, by Warren Chappell, from contemporary photographs by Matthew Brady and others.

INTRODUCTION

The Civil War is a sword cut across American history. Before it there is one United States, and after it another, and yet there is only one body, and the arteries run through. What songs they would have sung in New England, what romances written in the South, is unknown. An unborn future moulders with John Brown's body in the grave.

> The new mechanic birth
> No longer bound by toil
> To the unsparing soil
> Or the old furrow line,
> The great metallic heart
> Expanding West and East,

which is America today, knows little of its own past, has been taught only formalities of state rights or economic destiny. There has been little of that time-defeating literature conveying the emotional truth that makes *Henry V* better English history than a sober chronicle. The American poets and philosophers of the Golden Age of literature in the mid-century were aware of individuals and localities, but not of the nation. If Transcendentalism was too large for lyrics, it was also too local for a national drama. Even Whitman had to imagine a democracy of the future in order to get his theme. It is scarcely an exaggeration to say that one must skip from the empty rhetoric of the Columbiads, premature epics of a nation, to the satire of Sinclair Lewis in order to find a vital literature concerned with the great theme of a national life.

Yet for seventy years the Civil War has been waiting for its poet. As a theme it has richer possibilities than any other Western struggle since the seventeenth century, with the probable exceptions of the French, the Russian, and the Industrial Revolutions. Hardy resorted to tragic irony in order to lift the Napoleonic Wars above a complex of skill, disaster, and the breakdown of monarchy. But our Civil War is dramatic with a sharp and simple theme—karma: destiny as determined by irrevocable acts, a conflict of two civilizations bound together like twin enemies in a trap of their own making, the heavy payment of innocent men for the will of their ancestors, the fierce struggle of moral codes unlike though resemblant, the cruel consequence of an impersonal economics pouring like a rock slide over happy valleys.

Of course the troubled mid-century of the United States had to become a wake on the horizon before it could be written about effectively at all. The alliance of fanatic New England idealism and pushing economic energy which crushed the static civilization of the South had to find its blend and level in the Age of Material Comfort that followed, the vanquished South had to get done with sentimentalizing its past, before there could be more than lyric or melodrama written of the conflict as a whole.

It seems, too, that the Civil War was too modern in its aspects, by which I mean too much of a people's war, familiar, sordid, wide-reaching, disillusioning, to be made into literature by the old methods. It was not Shakespeare's kind of war, nor Addison's, nor Byron's, nor Tennyson's, nor Kipling's even. The age of plain people and scientific education had to pass through its naturalistic stage before Bull Run and slavery, Lincoln, Jeff Davis, and the psychology of cultures could be taken over into an intelligible literature.

And hence it is no derogation to Stephen Benét's broad and stirring saga, to say that time and events have made it possible. Neither he nor we could have known what a people's war meant before 1914–1918. A generation ago, before the United States became a Power and began to be described in terms less naïve than Manifest Destiny, it would have been impossible to make a unity of all this confusion. We did not know enough economics, could not get the rights and wrongs in perspective, would have been content either with odes on the North and pæans on the South, or with local color sketches like Stephen Crane's *The Red Badge of Courage.*

But that mid-century America is now as dead as the Past ever is. It is an Age, a Period, a Phase, still familiar but in no immediate sense Us. It is an analyzable America that might have become something different. It is heroic, wrong-headed, shameful, potent, and, like all Pasts, in a different mode from ours. It is a major premise for modern America, but active only in the results of the syllogism. We can see it now as we see the Revolutionary fathers, acutely and sympathetically, but as something familiar, yet strange, that lived before our times. And this is a prerequisite for successful studies of the Past. It must be a real Past for the imaginative artist, where he can reconstruct according to his own interests (since the Present only is alive), remaking a Crisis according to its significance for history, which means, of course, for him and for us.

And I think also that *John Brown's Body* owes quite as much to the wave of realism in literature that has rolled up between us and that past. It is both a tribute to the climax of realism, which was naturalism, and a sign of its passing. A romantic poem, rising to heights of eloquence, and singularly rich in passages of lyric sweetness, so that, unlike any of the American poetry of the last two decades, it moves the reader to emotional enthusiasm, it is beautiful as well as intricate, and has as much pathos as excitement, as much sentiment as intellectual analysis. And yet it is as realistic as it is romantic. The Jake Diefers and the Baileys and the Shippys, the prostitutes with Confederate flags on their garters, the rough-neck business of war, and the small-town emotions; the ease with which the poet gets off his high horse when Lee has ridden past on Traveller, so that he shall get it all in, the homely with the sublime, without losing his grip on the significance of the whole;—this he has learned from naturalistic fiction, from the Zolas, the Dreisers, the Andersons, the Wellses and the Bennetts, and also from the Frosts, the Lindsays, and the Masterses that Conservatives have been deploring.

And he has taken his zig-zag continuity, where, like pictures on a screen, or memories in the consciousness, the noble and the mean, the tragic and the funny, pass and break and are picked up again and dropped, from James Joyce and the movies, from the behaviorists and the impressionists. No, this poem could not have been written twenty years ago.

I am describing *John Brown's Body* rather than analyzing it, because I cannot with any justice analyze it in a limited space and describe it too. It has been widely read, and will be still more widely read, for it is not one of your *tours de force* of intellect and technique to be admired and then tucked away on the library shelf. It is a library of story telling itself, a poem extraordinarily rich in action as well as actors, vivid, varied, and so expressive of many men and moods that prose could never have carried its electric burden. Benét has as many voices as an organ. He has the art of suspense and the gift of movement which our intellectual poets definitely lack when they try to tell a story. He has a suavity of diction, when he wants it, which is dangerous in pure lyric but indispensable to a fine narrative poem. He knows how to raise the cloud no bigger than a man's hand with his opening scene on a slaver captained by a fanatic. He has the sense for drama which chooses as his protagonist, not Lincoln who carried through, but the tough-fibred individualist, John Brown, blind to immediate consequence, a stone of fate for hammering walls, Thoreau's John Brown who had the mad courage to put his conscience against reason, a man pre-doomed to failure, whose soul went marching on. He has the broad vision of the historian of the modern type, who considers vanity, greed, ignorance, the cotton in the fields, fear, things inanimate as well as animate, until history becomes as complex as life—and much too complex for a historian to strike into a unity. And yet, as the artist must, he holds to his line of significance—not slavery, not economic rivalry, not race prejudice, but the struggle of individuals caught in karma, Lincoln and Jefferson Davis, Lee and Grant, Ellyat of Connecticut, Wingate of Georgia, Bailey of Illinois, Jake Diefer of Pennsylvania, the runaway negro, Spade, Sally Dupré, the subtle Jew Benjamin, all fighting in the irresistible tide of events sweeping through a broken dam toward chaos, all touched somewhere, somehow by great issues.

This poem, indeed, is good history, but it is also good art. I

am not inclined to be apologetic with the poet for his nationalistic
theme—

> So, from a hundred visions, I make one,
> And out of darkness build my mocking sun.
> And should that task seem fruitless in the eyes
> Of those a different magic sets apart
> To see through the ice-crystal of the wise
> No nation but the nation that is Art,
> Their words are just. . . .
> Art has no nations—but the mortal sky
> Lingers like gold in immortality.
> This flesh was seeded from no foreign grain
> But Pennsylvania and Kentucky wheat,
> And it has soaked in California rain
> And five years tempered in New England sleet.

We shall have passed beyond the need of national art when we
shall have passed beyond nations, or rather, when the possibilities of a culture vibrant with home and traditions shall have been
exhausted. Art has no nations, but it must be born somewhere,
and the American must make his own his own before it can be
good for others. If great events of which our own people have
been part and parcel do not move us, there is little chance for a
great literature built upon the Arthurian legends or the League
of Nations.

Indeed it is the intense nationalism of *John Brown's Body* that
is perhaps responsible for its esthetic importance, which is not
equalled, I should say, by any recent American book. For Benét
is writing as Shakespeare wrote in his histories, and Racine in
his tragedies, and Vergil in the *Æneid,* on a great theme in which
he himself has a vested interest. He cannot, and he does not,
take the view of that modernistic literature from which he bor-
rows so much in technique, that the writer should be, as a young
modernist has recently said, a skilful reporter merely of phenom-
ena whose meaning he does not pretend to understand. His poem
is composed, significant, and bound together in a moral unity. For
here is the inconsequentiality, the uncertainness, the mingled
grossity and valor of life, the vividness of minute experience, all
organized by a moral significance which in this fateful period can

be shown to have given one meaning, at least, to the whole. It is the method and point of view of the great poems of the past—but this does not prove that it is wrong. His subject is a Past. On the present he does not speculate, but merely says "it is here." Perhaps only a fool expects to grasp the significance of a present, but certainly only an impressionist can write of life at all unless he tries to grasp the moral organization which makes it different from the mechanics of a coral reef.

For his poem, he has chosen a blank verse of five or six stresses, planed down almost to prose; often it is prose, and sometimes is written as such. Conservative readers have complained of this oscillation between metrical poetry, in which the rhythm is sharply marked, and the freer, rougher rhythms of prose. They have asked why *John Brown's Body,* like *The Idylls of the King,* should not have been written throughout in a regular verse form, where the lines were always scannable according to the rules of blank verse, and the tone of pure poetry was always maintained.

One might answer that the Civil War is by no means such a theme as the conflicts of King Arthur or the war between the Trojans and the Greeks. It is close to us. It is mingled high tragedy, humor, and sordidness. It is almost necessarily seen by a realistic age, like ours, in terms of realism as well as romance. There is no inherent reason why prose and verse should not be mingled or verse of high suavity with verse of a freer, rougher rhythm—especially in a dramatic poem. Shakespeare did it, and let lovers of Tennyson who complain of the drops toward prose of *John Brown's Body* imagine this work done throughout in the rather monotonous suavity of *The Idylls* and consider again their argument. Certainly Benét was well aware of what he was doing, and could very well have employed the melodious loveliness of the verse he uses in the episode of The Hiders throughout, if he had wished.

As it is, the style of his poem rises and falls with the emotions of his theme. But for his personal stories, the Georgian Wingates and Sally Dupré, Cudjo the negro butler, Ellyat the Connecticut intellectual, and the rest, there is an extraordinary variety of rhythmic movements. The versatility of his poetic style is unusual. He can do anything except the organ line in which blank verse reaches its highest powers, and perhaps for this reason the historical center of his poem is the least impressive portion, although an excellent foil for the lyric movements that surround it. Lincoln in meditation is more effective than all his accounts of Lincoln, and the silent mystery of Lee is less striking just because Lee is silent. Benét is at his best as a dramatic lyricist. Yet where most epic poets are weak, he is strong. The humorous realism of his soldiers is excellent, yet I like him best of all in those incidental narratives, touched or driven by great events yet shining with their own light of merely human interest. The Negroes are the truest I know in American poetry.

I feel that this survey of *John Brown's Body* is unusually inadequate, even for criticism which must always let so much more slip through its fingers than can be held. I should like to consider Benét's thoughtful study of Lincoln which preserves both his homeliness and his poetry, comment on his very interesting view of Jefferson Davis, the honest orator, weigh his analysis of the inner meaning of the conflict, and discuss his quite unexpected resolution of the whole tragedy into the triumph of a machine age that knows neither John Brown nor morality. Politically, it is a non-partisan poem, spiritually it is Northern. The fanaticism of the North as well as its commercialism he accepts as irrevocable; the romance of the South he makes as brittle as its charm and haunting melancholy are persuasive. The Connecticut Ellyat and the rough boys from Illinois and Pennsylvania are much more convincing than Wingate and his Black Horse Troop, because they have psychologies while the Southerners are chiefly manners and fate. This is not true of his women. Sally Dupré, next to Melora, is his best; the Northern women are shadows. The answer lies probably in his own experience and is not important. We are not far enough yet from the 1860's to view his Greeks and Trojans with even Homer's impartiality.

This poem is clearly a poem of the transition. In spite of the firm grip upon purpose and significance, it is too fluent for a classic taste, bursting out at corners, pouring and flashing and jumping and zig-zagging through wide margins, where, when we have got on top of all the fascinating new material that realism has been gathering for us, we shall be more selective, restrained, intense. There will be more in every line and less broadcast through pages. The margins of experience will be attained by sheer skill of imaginative suggestion rather than by excessive roaming back and forth in the story. But this poem could have been done successfully only this way now, and it is an immense credit to Benét that he has been able to recreate the rough and tumble, sweet and sour of an epoch with a modern imagination, and yet hold it all in one grand theme.

HENRY SEIDEL CANBY

INTRO-DUCTION

xvi

JOHN BROWN'S BODY

INVOCATION

American muse, whose strong and diverse heart
So many men have tried to understand
But only made it smaller with their art,
Because you are as various as your land,

As mountainous-deep, as flowered with blue rivers,
Thirsty with deserts, buried under snows,
As native as the shape of Navajo quivers,
And native, too, as the sea-voyaged rose.

Swift runner, never captured or subdued,
Seven-branched elk beside the mountain stream,
That half a hundred hunters have pursued
But never matched their bullets with the dream,

Where the great huntsmen failed, I set my sorry
And mortal snare for your immortal quarry.

You are the buffalo-ghost, the broncho-ghost
With dollar-silver in your saddle-horn,
The cowboys riding in from Painted Post,
The Indian arrow in the Indian corn,

And you are the clipped velvet of the lawns
Where Shropshire grows from Massachusetts sods,
The grey Maine rocks—and the war-painted dawns
That break above the Garden of the Gods.

The prairie-schooners crawling toward the ore
And the cheap car, parked by the station-door.

Where the skyscrapers lift their foggy plumes
Of stranded smoke out of a stony mouth
You are that high stone and its arrogant fumes,
And you are ruined gardens in the South

And bleak New England farms, so winter-white
Even their roofs look lonely, and the deep
The middle grainland where the wind of night
Is like all blind earth sighing in her sleep.

A friend, an enemy, a sacred hag
With two tied oceans in her medicine-bag.

They tried to fit you with an English song
And clip your speech into the English tale.
But, even from the first, the words went wrong,
The catbird pecked away the nightingale.

The homesick men begot high-cheekboned things
Whose wit was whittled with a different sound
And Thames and all the rivers of the kings
Ran into Mississippi and were drowned.

They planted England with a stubborn trust.
But the cleft dust was never English dust.

Stepchild of every exile from content
And all the disavouched, hard-bitten pack
Shipped overseas to steal a continent
With neither shirts nor honor to their back.

Pimping grandee and rump-faced regicide,
Apple-cheeked younkers from a windmill-square,
Puritans stubborn as the nails of Pride,
Rakes from Versailles and thieves from County Clare,

The black-robed priests who broke their hearts in vain
To make you God and France or God and Spain.

These were your lovers in your buckskin-youth.
And each one married with a dream so proud
He never knew it could not be the truth
And that he coupled with a girl of cloud.

And now to see you is more difficult yet
Except as an immensity of wheel
Made up of wheels, oiled with inhuman sweat
And glittering with the heat of ladled steel.

All these you are, and each is partly you,
And none is false, and none is wholly true.

So how to see you as you really are,
So how to suck the pure, distillate, stored
Essence of essence from the hidden star
And make it pierce like a riposting sword.

For, as we hunt you down, you must escape
And we pursue a shadow of our own
That can be caught in a magician's cape
But has the flatness of a painted stone.

Never the running stag, the gull at wing,
The pure elixir, the American thing.

And yet, at moments when the mind was hot
With something fierier than joy or grief,

JOHN
BROWN'S
BODY

JOHN
BROWN'S
BODY

6

When each known spot was an eternal spot
And every leaf was an immortal leaf,

I think that I have seen you, not as one,
But clad in diverse semblances and powers,
Always the same, as light falls from the sun,
And always different, as the differing hours.

Yet, through each altered garment that you wore
The naked body, shaking the heart's core.

All day the snow fell on that Eastern town
With its soft, pelting, little, endless sigh
Of infinite flakes that brought the tall sky down
Till I could put my hands in the white sky.

And taste cold scraps of heaven on my tongue
And walk in such a changed and luminous light
As gods inhabit when the gods are young.
All day it fell. And when the gathered night

Was a blue shadow cast by a pale glow
I saw you then, snow-image, bird of the snow.

And I have seen and heard you in the dry
Close-huddled furnace of the city street
When the parched moon was planted in the sky
And the limp air hung dead against the heat.

I saw you rise, red as that rusty plant,
Dizzied with lights, half-mad with senseless sound,
Enormous metal, shaking to the chant
Of a triphammer striking iron ground.

Enormous power, ugly to the fool,
And beautiful as a well-handled tool.

These, and the memory of that windy day
On the bare hills, beyond the last barbed wire,
When all the orange poppies bloomed one way
As if a breath would blow them into fire,

I keep forever, like the sea-lion's tusk
The broken sailor brings away to land,
But when he touches it, he smells the musk,
And the whole sea lies hollow in his hand.

So, from a hundred visions, I make one,
And out of darkness build my mocking sun.

And should that task seem fruitless in the eyes
Of those a different magic sets apart
To see through the ice-crystal of the wise
No nation but the nation that is Art,

Their words are just. But when the birchbark-call
Is shaken with the sound that hunters make
The moose comes plunging through the forest-wall
Although the rifle waits beside the lake.

Art has no nations—but the mortal sky
Lingers like gold in immortality.

This flesh was seeded from no foreign grain
But Pennsylvania and Kentucky wheat,
And it has soaked in California rain
And five years tempered in New England sleet

To strive at last, against an alien proof
And by the changes of an alien moon,
To build again that blue, American roof
Over a half-forgotten battle-tune

And call unsurely, from a haunted ground,
Armies of shadows and the shadow-sound.

In your Long House there is an attic-place
Full of dead epics and machines that rust,
And there, occasionally, with casual face,
You come awhile to stir the sleepy dust;

Neither in pride nor mercy, but in vast
Indifference at so many gifts unsought,

JOHN
BROWN'S
BODY

The yellowed satins, smelling of the past,
And all the loot the lucky pirates brought.

I only bring a cup of silver air,
Yet, in your casualness, receive it there.

Receive the dream too haughty for the breast,
Receive the words that should have walked as bold
As the storm walks along the mountain-crest
And are like beggars whining in the cold.

The maimed presumption, the unskilful skill,
The patchwork colors, fading from the first,
And all the fire that fretted at the will
With such a barren ecstasy of thirst.

Receive them all—and should you choose to touch them
With one slant ray of quick, American light,
Even the dust will have no power to smutch them,
Even the worst will glitter in the night.

If not—the dry bones littered by the way
May still point giants toward their golden prey.

PRELUDE—THE SLAVER

H e closed the Bible carefully, putting it down
      As if his fingers loved it.

                              Then he turned.
"Mr. Mate."
            "Yes, sir."
                        The captain's eyes held a shadow.
"I think, while this weather lasts," he said, after a pause,
"We'd better get them on deck as much as we can.
They keep better that way. Besides," he added, unsmiling,
"She's begun to stink already. You've noticed it?"

The mate nodded, a boyish nod of half-apology,
"And only a week out, too, sir."
                              "Yes," said the skipper.
His eyes looked into themselves. "Well. The trade," he said,

"The trade's no damn perfume-shop." He drummed with his
    fingers.
"Seem to be quiet tonight," he murmured, at last.
"Oh yes sir, quiet enough." The mate flushed. "Not
What you'd call quiet at home but—quiet enough."

"Um," said the skipper. "What about the big fellow?"

"Tarbarrel, sir? The man who says he's a king?
He was praying to something—it made the others restless.
Mr. Olsen stopped it."
                    "I don't like that," said the skipper.

"It was only an idol, sir."
                    "Oh."
                              "A stone or something."
"Oh."
        "But he's a bad one, sir—a regular sullen one—
He—eyes in the dark—like a cat's—enough to give you—"
The mate was young. He shivered. "The creeps," he said.

"We've had that kind," said the skipper. His mouth was hard
Then it relaxed. "Damn cheating Arabe!" he said,
"I told them I'd take no more of their pennyweight kings,
Worth pounds to look at, and then when you get them aboard
Go crazy so they have to be knocked on the head
Or else just eat up their hearts and die in a week
Taking up room for nothing."

The mate hardly heard him, thinking of something else.
"I'm afraid we'll lose some more of the women," he said.
"Well, they're a scratch lot," said the skipper, "Any sickness?"

"Just the usual, sir."
                    "But nothing like plague or—"
                                        "No sir."

"The Lord is merciful," said the skipper.
His voice was wholly sincere—an old ship's bell
Hung in the steeple of a meeting-house
With all New England and the sea's noise in it.

"Well, you'd better take another look-see, Mr. Mate."
The mate felt his lips go dry. "Aye aye, sir," he said,
Wetting his lips with his tongue. As he left the cabin
He heard the Bible being opened again.

Lantern in hand, he went down to the hold.
Each time he went he had a trick of trying
To shut the pores of his body against the stench
By force of will, by thinking of salt and flowers,
But it was always useless.
                                He kept thinking:
When I get home, when I get a bath and clean food,
When I've gone swimming out beyond the Point
In that cold green, so cold it must be pure
Beyond the purity of a dissolved star,
When I get my shore-clothes on, and one of those shirts
Out of the linen-closet that smells of lavender,
Will my skin smell black even then, will my skin smell black?

The lantern shook in his hand.
                                This was black, here,
This was black to see and feel and smell and taste,
The blackness of black, with one weak lamp to light it
As ineffectually as a firefly in Hell,
And, being so, should be silent.
                                But the hold
Was never silent.
                        There was always that breathing.
Always that thick breathing, always those shivering cries.

A few of the slaves
Knew English—at least the English for water and Jesus.
"I'm dying." "Sick." "My name Caesar."
                                        Those who knew
These things, said these things now when they saw the lantern
Mechanically, as tamed beasts answer the whipcrack.
Their voices beat at the light like heavy moths.
But most made merely liquid or guttural sounds
Meaningless to the mate, but horribly like
The sounds of palateless men or animals trying
To talk through a human throat.

                              The mate was used
To the confusion of limbs and bodies by now.
At first it had made him think of the perturbed
Blind coil of blacksnakes thawing on a rock
In the bleak sun of Spring, or Judgment Day
Just after the first sounding of the trump
When all earth seethes and crumbles with the slow
Vast, mouldy resurrection of the dead.
But he had passed such fancies.
                              He must see
As much as he could. He couldn't see very much.
They were too tightly packed but—no plague yet,
And all the chains were fast. Then he saw something.
The woman was asleep but her baby was dead.
He wondered whether to take it from her now.
No, it would only rouse the others. Tomorrow.
He turned away with a shiver.
                              His glance fell
On the man who said he had been a king, the man
Called Tarbarrel, the image of black stone
Whose eyes were savage gods.
                              The huge suave muscles
Rippled like stretching cats as he changed posture,
Magnificence in chains that yet was ease.
The smolder in those eyes. The steady hate.

The mate made himself stare till the eyes dropped.
Then he turned back to the companionway.
His forehead was hot and sweaty. He wiped it off,
But then the rough cloth of his sleeve smelt black.

The captain shut the Bible as he came in.
"Well, Mister Mate?"
                              "All quiet, sir."
                              The captain
Looked at him sharply. "Sit down," he said in a bark.
The mate's knees gave as he sat. "It's—hot down there,"
He said, a little weakly, wanting to wipe
His face again, but knowing he'd smell that blackness
Again, if he did.

"Takes you that way, sometimes,"
Said the captain, not unkindly, "I remember
Back in the twenties."
                        Something hot and strong
Bit the mate's throat. He coughed.
                                    "There," said the captain,
Putting the cup down. "You'll feel better now.
You're young for this trade, Mister, and that's a fact."

The mate coughed and didn't answer, much too glad
To see the captain change back to himself
From something made of steam, to want to talk.
But, after a while, he heard the captain talking,
Half to himself.
                    "It's a fact, that," he was saying,
"They've even made a song of me—ever heard it?"
The mate shook his head, quickly, "Oh yes you have.
You know how it goes." He cleared his throat and hummed:

> *"Captain Ball was a Yankee slaver,*
> *Blow, blow, blow the man down!*
> *He traded in niggers and loved his Saviour,*
> *Give me some time to blow the man down."*

The droning chanty filled the narrow cabin
An instant with grey Massachusetts sea,
Wave of the North, wave of the melted ice,
The hard salt-sparkles on the harder rock.
The stony islands.
                    Then it died away.
"Well," said the captain, "if that's how it strikes them—
They mean it bad but I don't take it bad.
I get my sailing-orders from the Lord."
He touched the Bible. "And it's down there, Mister,
Down there in black and white—the sons of Ham—
Bondservants—sweat of their brows." His voice trailed off
Into texts. "I tell you, Mister," he said fiercely,
"The pay's good pay, but it's the Lord's work, too.
We're spreading the Lord's seed—spreading his seed—"

His hand made the outflung motion of a sower
And the mate, staring, seemed to hear the slight
Patter of fallen seeds on fertile ground,
Black, shining seeds, robbed from a black king's storehouse,
Falling and falling on American earth
With light, inexorable patter and fall,
To strike, lie silent, quicken.
                        Till the Spring
Came with its weeping rains, and the ground bore
A blade, a shadow-sapling, a tree of shadow,
A black-leaved tree whose trunk and roots were shadow,
A tree shaped like a yoke, growing and growing
Until it blotted all the seamen's stars.

Horses of anger trampling, horses of anger,
Trampling behind the sky in ominous cadence,
Beat of the heavy hooves like metal on metal,
Trampling something down. . . .
                        Was it they, was it they?
Or was it cold wind in the leaves of the shadow-tree
That made such grievous music?

                Oh Lordy Je-sus
                Won't you come and find me?
                They put me in jail, Lord,
                Way down in the jail.
                Won't you send me a pro-phet
                Just one of your prophets
                Like Moses and Aaron
                To get me some bail?

                I'm feeling poorly
                Yes, mighty poorly,
                I ain't got no strength, Lord,
                I'm all trampled down.
                So send me an angel
                Just any old angel
                To give me a robe, Lord,
                And give me a crown.

Oh Lordy Je-sus
It's a long time comin'
It's a long time co-o-min'
That Jubilee time.
We'll wait and we'll pray, Lord,
We'll wait and we'll pray, Lord,
But it's a long time, Lord,
Yes, it's a long time.

The dark sobbing ebbed away.
The captain was still talking. "Yes," he said,
"And yet we treat 'em well enough. There's no one
From Salem to the Guinea Coast can say
They lose as few as I do." He stopped.
                              "Well, Mister?"
The mate arose. "Good night sir and—"
                              "Good night."

The mate went up on deck. The breeze was fresh.
There were the stars, steady. He shook himself
Like a dog coming out of water and felt better.
Six weeks, with luck, and they'd be back in port
And he could draw his pay and see his girl.
Meanwhile, it wasn't his watch, so he could sleep.
The captain still below, reading that Bible. . . .
Forget it—and the noises, still half-heard—
He'd have to go below to sleep, this time,
But after, if the weather held like this,
He'd have them sling a hammock up on deck.
You couldn't smell the black so much on deck
And so you didn't dream it when you slept.

BOOK ONE

Jack Ellyat had been out all day alone,
    Except for his new gun and Ned, the setter,
The old wise dog with Autumn in his eyes,
Who stepped the fallen leaves so delicately
They barely rustled. Ellyat trampled them down
Crackling, like cast-off skins of fairy snakes.
He'd meant to hunt, but he had let the gun
Rest on his shoulder.

                            It was enough to feel
The cool air of the last of Indian summer
Blowing continually across his cheek
And watch the light distill its water of gold
As the sun dropped.

                            Here was October, here
Was ruddy October, the old harvester,

Wrapped like a beggared sachem in a coat
Of tattered tanager and partridge feathers,
Scattering jack-o-lanterns everywhere
To give the field-mice pumpkin-colored moons.
His red clay pipe had trailed across the land
Staining the trees with colors of the sumach:
East, West, South, North, the ceremonial fume
Blue and enchanted as the soul of air
Drifted its incense.
                    Incense of the wild,
Incense of earth fulfilled, ready to sleep
The stupefied dark slumber of the bear
All winter, underneath a frozen star.

Jack Ellyat felt that turning of the year
Stir in his blood like drowsy fiddle-music
And knew he was glad to be Connecticut-born
And young enough to find Connecticut winter
Was a black pond to cut with silver skates
And not a scalping-knife against the throat.
He thought the thoughts of youth, idle and proud.

        Since I was begotten
        My father's grown wise
        But he has forgotten
        The wind in the skies.
        I shall not grow wise.

        Since I have been growing
        My uncle's got rich.
        He spends his time sowing
        A bottomless ditch.
        I will not grow rich.

        For money is sullen
        And wisdom is sly,
        But youth is the pollen
        That blows through the sky
        And does not ask why.

O wisdom and money
How can you requite
The honey of honey
That flies in that flight?
The useless delight?

JOHN
BROWN'S
BODY

So, with his back against a tree, he stared
At the pure, golden feathers in the West
Until the sunset flowed into his heart
Like a slow wave of honey-dropping dew
Murmuring from the other side of Sleep.
There was a fairy hush
Everywhere. Even the setter at his feet
Lay there as if the twilight had bewitched
His russet paws into two russet leaves,
A dog of russet leaves who did not stir a hair.

Then something broke the peace.
Like wind it was, the flutter of rising wind,
But then it grew until it was the rushing
Of winged stallions, distant and terrible,
Trampling beyond the sky.
                                        The hissing charge
Of lightless armies of angelic horse
Galloping down the stars.
                                        There were no words
In that implacable and feathery thunder,
And yet there must have been, or Ellyat's mind
Caught them like broken arrows out of the air.

Thirteen sisters beside the sea,
(Have a care, my son.)
Builded a house called Liberty
And locked the doors with a stately key.
None should enter it but the free.
(Have a care, my son.)

The walls are solid as Plymouth Rock.
(Rock can crumble, my son.)
The door of seasoned New England stock.